Old DUMBARTON
by
John Hood

For centuries Dumbarton was largely confined to an area along the River Leven, but from the late 1800s expansion took place away from the river to the east in the 'Newtown' or, as it is now known, Dumbarton East. By the early 1900s, when this photograph was taken, further development had taken place beyond Newtown towards Dumbuck. One such development was the infamous works of Alexander Shiel's Kosmoid Limited, the rectangular building to the left of the picture, which opened just off the Glasgow Road in 1904. In addition to manufacturing weldless steel tubes, the works reputedly experimented in turning base metals into gold. It is said that a sum of £250,000 was poured into the project by various well-respected local figures such as Lord Kelvin, Lord Overtoun, and the shipbuilder, James Denny. However, the experiment was quickly discredited and, as a result, the works closed down in May 1907.

© John Hood, 1999
First published in the United Kingdom, 1999,
by Stenlake Publishing Ltd.
01290 551122
www.stenlake.co.uk

ISBN 9781840330588

Printed by
Blissetts, Roslin Road, Acton, W3 8DH

**The publishers regret that they cannot supply
copies of any pictures featured in this book.**

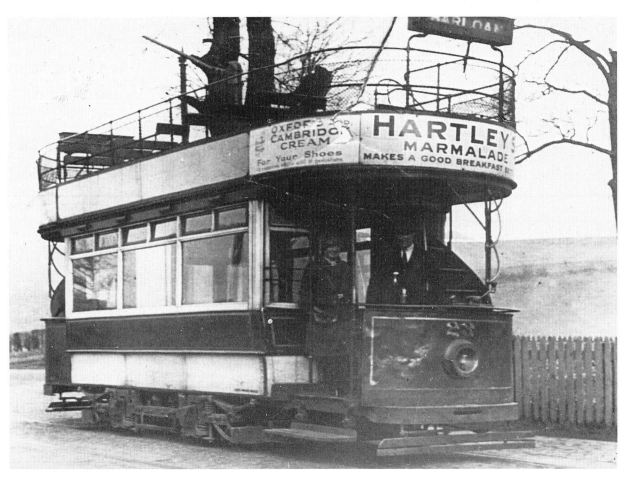

When tramway operations in Dumbarton began six electric trams were purchased at a cost of £700 each. Each double-decker four-window saloon tram seated 34 upstairs and 22 downstairs. The trams were painted chocolate and cream with the burgh coat of arms on the side. A second batch of trams, purchased when the system was extended the following year, were open-top double-decker three-window saloons – this model seating one less upstairs! From 1 January 1908 the trams came under the control of a subsidiary company, the Dumbarton Burgh & County Tramways Co. Ltd, and the livery then changed to green and cream. When the one-and-a-half mile branch line from Alexandria to Jamestown was opened in February 1909, the company bought another four open-topped double-decker trams from Glasgow Corporation which they then converted into single-deckers.

INTRODUCTION

The Burgh of Dumbarton grew up in the shadow of the 240-foot high Dumbarton Rock. The latter, one of the most prominent landmarks on the Clyde, was known in ancient times as Alcluith, and to the later Gaelic speaking Scots of neighbouring Dalriada the settlement on the Rock was known as Dun Breatann – the fort of the Britons. Until 1034 it was the capital of the British kingdom of Strathclyde, and by the thirteenth century it was the principal town within the Celtic Earldom of Lennox. It was created a Royal Burgh in 1222 by Alexander II and it was at this time the castle was acquired by the Crown for use as a royal fortress.

From the fourteenth century onwards, Dumbarton enjoyed a thriving local trade as well as trading links with France, Ireland and England. It was also a strategically important gateway for controlling the Western Highlands and Islands. Throughout the fifteenth and sixteenth centuries, the local Earls of Lennox became prominent in Scottish politics. In 1548 the infant Mary, Queen of Scots sought refuge in the castle, staying for two years until she embarked from there to France. She visited the castle again in 1563 and during the troubles which followed her abdication it was held for her by her supporters until it was captured under the orders of the Earl of Lennox, who had become regent in Mary's place.

In 1609 King James VI granted the burgh a new charter that reaffirmed all the trading rights and privileges conferred on it by the 1222 Charter. Of particular importance was the burgh's right to levy anchorage dues on all ships on the Clyde. However, this right was lost in 1658 and, together with the burgh's rejection of a proposal by Glasgow to develop Dumbarton harbour as a port for Glasgow, sent its shipping trade into dramatic decline by the end of the century.

It wasn't until the beginning of the nineteenth century that Dumbarton's prosperity returned and this was largely due to its glass-making and shipbuilding industries. The closure of the Dumbarton Glassworks in 1831 thus had a major impact on the burgh's economy and by 1850 shipbuilding had become its principal industry. By then, largely due to the energy of the Denny and the Macmillan families, Dumbarton could boast five local shipyards and several associated engineering works, forges and foundries.

This period, from 1850 to the end of the century, saw great changes within the burgh that affected all classes. With plentiful employment, the population increased from 5,445 to 14,319 and new suburbs were created across the Leven at Kirktonhill and to the east in the Newtown. Further prosperity came in 1858 when a railway line was constructed linking Dumbarton with Glasgow, although, paradoxically, this brought about the decline of Dumbarton harbour.

By the turn of the twentieth century only two shipyards were still in operation. The local economy was boosted when the American firm of Babcock & Wilcox opened their factory, but the 1930s saw a further decline when Macmillan's Shipyard, Paul's Engineering Works and Dennystown Brassworks all closed. Nevertheless, later in the decade the Canadian firm of Hiram Walker & Son took over the old Macmillan Yard, and Blackburn (Dumbarton) opened a factory to build, initially, Sunderland Flying Boats. In 1946 an industrial estate was opened at Strathleven which attracted a diverse range of firms including Burroughs Adding Machines and Westclox. However, the end of over one hundred years of shipbuilding in Dumbarton came in 1963, with the closure of Denny's Leven Yard.

This rapid industrial growth from 1850 onwards inevitably led to overcrowding in many parts of the burgh. In 1911 it was estimated that 55% of the population lived in one or two-roomed houses that lacked indoor sanitation. After the passing of the 1919 Addison Act to improve working class accommodation, the burgh began to deal with this problem by initiating a programme of new building and slum clearance. The Brucehill estate on Cardross Road was built at this time and further large-scale re-housing programmes were started in the late 1940s at Bellsmyre, Garshake and Castlehill. Within the old burgh area itself there was almost continuous re-development, in the 1950s and particularly throughout the sixties with the improvement of access to the Quay (and landscaping of the resultant area) and construction of a new town centre. In the 1970s new by-pass roads and a new bridge were built to improve the flow of traffic through the town, so that today the burgh has a decidedly different look from the way it was captured in the photographs of in this book.

By the mid-1930s the Glasgow Road area had been progressively developed. The Kosmoid works had been briefly taken over by the Dumbarton Weldless Tube Co. Ltd. and thereafter, in 1910, by the American firm, Babcock & Wilcox, who specialised in the manufacture of boilers. Until their demise in 1965, Babcock & Wilcox was a major employer in the area, extending their factory on Glasgow Road on several occasions. They built villas on Glasgow Road for their managers and cottages at Geils Avenue (pictured bottom right) for their workmen. Further development of this area took place when gas production for Dumbarton and the surrounding district was located nearby. The use of gas was first introduced into Dumbarton around 1832 and replaced the oil lamps used to light shops and streets. From 1873 to 1930 the production of gas was undertaken by the Burgh Council, latterly at premises on Glasgow Road, but in 1954 a new Scottish Gas Board Works was built to the west of the Babcock factory.

Geils Avenue takes its name from one of the older Dumbarton families who acquired the estate of Dumbuck in 1815. In 1843, following the death of Colonel Andrew Geils at Dumbuck House, his fifth son succeeded to the estate in tragic circumstances as his four elder brothers drowned at sea while travelling from Ceylon to Britain to be educated at home. Behind the cottages is the 547 foot high Dumbuck Hill ('the hill of the deer'). Higher than its more famous neighbour, Dumbarton Rock, its summit was occupied by Bonnie Prince Charlie's forces during the 1745 rebellion in an attempt to threaten Dumbarton Castle.

Around 1860 much of the area known as East Bridgend was open fields, with a few scattered mansions on or near Glasgow Road. However, when this picture was taken in 1934, the area had become highly developed. Prior to the establishment of Denny's Leven Shipyard in 1867, the area at the base of Dumbarton Rock was occupied by Castlegreen House, which was owned by Peter Denny. In 1881 the house was bought by the Denny company and demolished to allow the Leven Shipyard to occupy a site extending from Castle Street to the castle itself. In 1937 the Barge Park site immediately east of the shipyard was laid out for the manufacture of Sunderland flying boats by Blackburn, who, from 1945 to 1948, switched to the manufacture of prefabricated aluminium housing, affectionately known as 'prefabs'. The factory closed in 1960. In the background, beyond the Leven Shipyard, are the suburbs of Castlegreen and Knoxland, nowadays part of Dumbarton East.

67855. (IV)

The Dennys were one of the great Dumbarton shipbuilding dynasties. In the mid-1800s, four out of the burgh's five shipyards belonged to members of this family. From 1845 to 1867 they built ships at the Woodyard but afterwards moved across the river to their new shipyard, pictured here in 1909 complete with stocks and fitting-out basin. This shipyard was built partly on the site of the earlier Victoria Shipyard and partly on reclaimed land. Before closure in 1963, Denny launched many fine ships, including the *Paris* which was the fastest passenger ship of her size when she was launched in 1913. Other notable ships included the *Rotomahana*, the first steel ocean-going steamer; the *King Edward,* the world's first turbine-engined passenger ship; and the *Shamrock II* which was built in 1901 for Sir Thomas Lipton's Americas Cup bid.

The new suburb of Knoxland in Newtown was built around the site of the former Knoxland House and grounds which in the 1860s had stood alone in Glasgow Road. Like nearby Castlegreen House, Knoxland House was acquired by the Dennys and later demolished to enable the area to be re-developed for housing for their workers. Knoxland Square was presented by Peter Denny to the town in 1890 and was a prominent feature of the new suburb. In this view looking east, young children are playing on the paved open-plan square, with Knoxland School, Knoxland Parish Church (both built in 1884) and the bandstand in the background. The school was demolished in 1974 (now replaced by Knoxland Primary School, built further west on Glasgow Road) and the church and bandstand have also gone.

From the 1880s further housing to the north of Knoxland on Glasgow Road was provided by the Dumbarton Equitable Co-operative Society and the Dumbarton Building Society. Many of the properties seen here date from this period and most survive today. Initially, the most prominent building on Glasgow Road was the handsome Dumbarton Equitable Co-operative Society building which was erected in 1879 at the corner of Park Street. A notable feature of the building was its large clock, popularly known as McQueen's Clock because it was maintained by a Mr McQueen, a Co-op employee. In early 1941, however, Dumbarton was attacked by German bombers and the building was among the casualties. Today, the site is occupied by a modern Co-operative Society store. In the background, behind the tram, is Dumbarton East Railway Station and East End Park, which was gifted to the burgh in 1914 by Dr J. Douglas White and Peter Denny.

Despite expansion to the east and west, the 'old' burgh still had a decidedly congested look by the time of this 1927 photograph. This was mainly due to geographical reasons, clearly demonstrated by an 1818 map which shows the River Leven surrounding the burgh on three sides. To the west, beyond Dumbarton Bridge, the River Leven turned back on its course and until 1859 regularly flooded the area called the Broad Meadow (nowadays partially occupied by Dumbarton Common). In the sixteenth century, a dyke, known locally as the 'Bishop's water-gang', had been constructed by the Collegiate Church to hold back the Leven, but gradually it fell into disrepair and around 1580 the Leven burst its banks and flooded the Broad Meadow. The flooded areas or 'drowned lands' were not reclaimed until a railway line was laid through the burgh in the mid-1800s. In the foreground, alongside the River Leven, is Macmillan's Dockyard which closed in 1930.

From early times, Dumbarton was the site of a strategically important fortress which became a royal castle in the Middle Ages. During the Scottish Wars of Independence it was said to be the prison of William Wallace before he was sent to London for trial and execution, and after the Scottish defeat at Halidon Hill in 1333 it sheltered Robert Bruce's son, David II, and his young queen, Joan. In 1548, after the Battle of Pinkie, it protected the infant Mary, Queen of Scots until she could be safely taken to France. With the death of Oliver Cromwell in 1658 its importance as a fortress declined but its defences were later strengthened in the eighteenth century when a French invasion was feared. Today the castle is a popular visitor attraction and is in the care of Historic Scotland.

In earlier times, Dumbarton Castle was completely surrounded by water several times each day and had its main entrance to the north. Later, after land reclamation, a new main entrance, shown here, was built on the south side facing the River Clyde. To accommodate this change, the fortifications to the north, including the late fifteenth century Wallace Tower, were considerably altered and very little of the medieval castle survives today. Beyond the outer entrance walls are the five cannons of the King George Battery and the Governor's House, within which is housed the Dunbartonshire Volunteers Museum. The Garden Terrace alongside the house marks the site of the former Chapel of St Patrick which was demolished in the sixteenth century. The site of the Clyde Restaurant is now occupied by the Rock Bowling Club.

A panoramic view taken from Dumbarton Rock in the late 1940s. In the foreground is the River Leven at Sandpoint and further up, beyond Dumbarton Bridge, are the suburbs of West Bridgend and Dennystown. Behind Sandpoint is the Woodyard, used for shipbuilding from the early 1800s. This was Denny's original shipyard and it was here that work began on the world famous tea clipper, *Cutty Sark*. Prominent in the centre of the picture is Hiram Walker & Sons' Dumbarton Distillery. The Canadian firm (owned by Allied Distillers Ltd since 1988) came to Dumbarton in 1938 and on the site of Macmillan's shipyard built what was then Europe's largest and most modern distillery. It is estimated that over a million bricks were used in the building and at one time Hiram Walker & Sons produced 10% of all exported whisky in Scotland.

The *Comet* (named after one which appeared in 1811) was designed by Henry Bell, the first provost of Helensburgh, and was built in Port Glasgow to provide a passenger service between his town and Glasgow. It was one of the world's earliest steamboats and in August 1812 made its maiden journey from Port Glasgow to the Broomielaw in Glasgow in three and a half hours. Although it was an immediate success, rival vessels soon appeared on the river and it wasn't long before the *Comet* proved unequal to the competition. It eventually left the Clyde to operate on the West Highland run and sank off Craignish Point during a return voyage from Fort William in 1820.

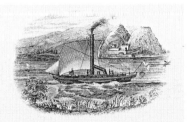

The *Comet* revolutionised transport on the Clyde and the popularity of the river boats is noted in the burgh's entry in the *New Statistical Account* (1839) where it is remarked that 'the chief means of travelling are on the steamboats on the Clyde which pass up and down almost every hour of the day'. The Dumbarton shipbuilding firms were among the foremost designers of Clyde steamers and Denny's Shipyard launched many famous steamers including the *TSS Queen Mary II* pictured here. She was actually launched in 1933 as the *Queen Mary* but following the launch in 1934 of Clydebank's great passenger liner, the *RMS Queen Mary*, the ship's owners agreed to change her name. When the *RMS Queen Mary* was withdrawn from service, however, the *Queen Mary II* reverted to her original name.

Formerly known as Kirk Vennel, Church Street was one of the principal streets in the old burgh and ran in a northerly direction from the High Street to Bonhill Road. To the left of the picture, at Church Place, is the High Street United Presbyterian Church which stood between 1826 and 1957. Alongside the church is the Town Mission which was built around 1873 and which later became an occupational centre for the unemployed before demolition in 1963. The tree beside the Mission is on the site of the entrance to the old Grammar School and is also the former site of the College Bow. On the opposite side of the street is the Burgh Hall and Academy, erected in 1865 by public subscription. Beyond the Burgh Hall, the tower of the Denny Institute, which opened in 1892 as a memorial to the shipbuilder William Denny, can just be seen above the Windsor Buildings.

The stone Arch, popularly known as the College Bow, was a prominent feature of Church Street for many years and marked the entrance to the Collegiate Church of St Mary. The church was founded in 1453 by Isabella, Countess of Lennox and Duchess of Albany, who suffered the tragic double loss of her husband and father in 1425 when both were executed on the orders of James I. She herself was imprisoned for a time, but thereafter lived quietly in her castle at Inchmurrin on Loch Lomond. With the exception of the Arch, the last traces of the church and associated buildings were removed when the present Dumbarton Central Station was built on its site. Over the years the Arch has been moved twice, firstly in 1850 to the foot of Church Street, and then in 1907 to the grounds of the newly-built Municipal Buildings where it stands today.

Now serving as the Sheriff Court, the County Buildings were built between 1824 and 1826, with north and south wings added between 1895 and 1898. The middle section, the County Hall, was the scene of a riot in 1831 which broke out after voting had taken place in the local election. Behind the buildings stood Dumbarton Prison which was closed in 1883. It was then used as a store by the council and demolished in the 1970s to make way for the by-pass. The County Buildings themselves eventually proved inadequate for the council and it moved to new offices in Crosslet in 1965.

Over the years, local pipe bands have enjoyed major recognition and here, pictured in 1906, is a very distinguished looking Dumbarton Pipe Band resplendent in full regalia. The reverse of this early postcard records an engagement for the band to play at the Dumbarton Glen Concert in Murroch Glen on Saturday, 9 June 1906. Over the last fifty years, successive pipe bands have continued the fine tradition of their predecessors. In 1950, for example, the Lennox Pipe Band competed with distinction in the Glasgow, European and World Championships, and in 1972 the Dumbarton District Pipe Band was placed first in the Grade 2 Drumming Section, thereby earning the right to claim the title of World Champions in that category.

Church Place is located at the junction of Church Street, Castle Street and High Street. The latter is still the principal thoroughfare in the old burgh and runs in a crescent shape towards Townhead, following the course of the Leven which still floods it occasionally. To the left of the picture Old Dumbarton Parish Church can just be seen, while beyond the trees is the roof of the office building of Macmillan's Shipyard (later Hiram Walker's Dumbarton Distillery office). For a while this building housed the local Procurator Fiscal's office but is presently lying empty. On the opposite corner is the High Street United Presbyterian Church and just short of Church Place an open-top tram is standing at the High Street terminus where the tramway routes diverged.

Until Church Place was redeveloped in the 1960s, Castle Street, which in the picture leads off to the right, was a continuation eastwards of High Street and led, in turn, to Glasgow Road. It is now, however, a short cul-de-sac which ends at the entrance to the Scottish Maritime Museum's Denny Tank Museum. The tenement on the left is on Hodge's Corner and was built in 1885-86. This is still standing, but the buildings beyond it and the brick buildings opposite have gone, the latter replaced by the Allied Distillers Ltd bottling complex. Near the head of Castle Street, at Castle Terrace, is an arched doorway – a remnant of the façade of the Leven Shipyard Experimental Tank (nowadays referred to as the Denny Tank). Above the doorway there is a tablet relief of the head of William Froude commemorating his work as 'the greatest of experimenters and investigators in hydrodynamics'.

Looking towards Castle Street, the eastern end of High Street is dominated by the imposing Old Parish Church. This is the oldest church in Dumbarton and was built in 1811 to replace a medieval church of St Mary which stood on the same site. The church includes some fine stained glass memorial windows dedicated to James and Catherine Denny and gifted by the family in 1938. There were no interments in the old churchyard after 1856 and the graves were exhumed in the 1970s to allow new church halls to be built to the rear of the church. Following amalgamation with the neighbouring North and High Churches, the church was re-named Riverside Parish Church. To the left is St Augustine's Episcopal Church, designed by Sir Robert Rowand Anderson; its wedding register includes the names of the Glasgow architect Charles Rennie Mackintosh and his wife Margaret.

Car Terminus, High Street, Dumbarton

Perhaps the most dramatic changes brought about by modern redevelopment have occurred in the High Street. For example, much of the north side from the junction with College Street eastwards to the Dumbarton Equitable Society Buildings were pulled down in the 1960s to make way for a modern town centre complex. Surprisingly, the buildings on the left of this 1909 photograph have largely survived. The area beyond St Augustine's Church has been completely redeveloped and the properties to the rear of the buildings also went with the construction of St Mary's Way.

The High Street was a popular route for processions and here the Helenslee Juvenile Branch of the Ancient Order of Shepherds are at the eastern end of the street, heading towards Bridge Street. The Helenslee Juvenile Branch was the junior section of the Pride of Leven Lodge which was formed in 1868. Both sections, together with the North Briton's Lodge No.1, held their meetings in the Town Mission Hall in nearby Church Street. Another lodge, the Heart and Hand Lodge, met in High Street United Presbyterian Church Hall, also in Church Street. A gothic obelisk in Dumbarton Cemetery commemorates both the formation of the Pride of Leven Lodge and the introduction of the Ancient Shepherds Friendly Society into Scotland.

Many of the rather grand properties on High Street, here viewed from the Cross, have long been swept away by successive redevelopments. Amongst these were the Lennox Temperance Hotel (on the south side of the street) and, opposite, the Mackenzie House and the King's Arms Inn. The property, which included Walker's Close, was replaced in 1903 by a more modern building which incorporated a pend leading to the United Free High Church Hall. In 1966 this itself was replaced by a complex of buildings forming the new town centre.

River Leven and Ship yards, Dumbarton.

Shipbuilding reached a peak in Dumbarton in the mid-nineteenth century when there were five yards in operation: Archibald Macmillan's Dockyard, William Denny's Woodyard, Alexander Denny's Albert Yard, Archibald Denny & John MacLean's yard between the river and the Parish Church, and, finally, Peter Denny & Daniel Rankin's Victoria Yard. The oldest was Macmillan's which was established east of Dumbarton Quay in 1834. The firm quickly gained a reputation for building the largest and fastest sailing ships in Scotland, although it was Scott & Linton at nearby Sandpoint who laid down the hull of Dumbarton's best known vessel, the *Cutty Sark*. Macmillan's was closed in the 1930s when the industry was slimmed down by the government-appointed National Shipbuilders Security Ltd.

This 1947 view of the High Street, looking west from Churchyard Lane, will probably be more recognisable to readers, although some of the properties on the north side would later make way for the new town centre which finally opened in 1969, having been first proposed fourteen years earlier. To the bottom left of the picture is Churchyard Lane which extended from the parish church down to the river and Macmillan's shipyard. During redevelopment of the Quay area, the lane was later altered to form Riverside Lane and give improved access to the old Dumbarton Quay area. The distinctive Burton's building at Quay Street is prominent in the distance.

High Street at the Cross, with the junctions of Quay Street and College Street on the left and right respectively. The white-sided building on the left beyond Quay Street is Glencairn House, one of the oldest buildings in Dumbarton. Dating from 1623, it was owned by the Earls of Glencairn. For many years it was the centre of everyday life in Dumbarton and was where proclamations were made and public meetings held. Since 1923 it has been owned by the local authority, who had it substantially altered in the mid-1920s. These alterations are most evident in the lower portion of the building and include the three distinctive exterior arches. The tenement directly opposite Glencairn House stands on the site of an earlier property known locally as the 'Holy Land' because, despite having been damaged by fire several times, it never completely burned down.

Burton's Gents Outfitters opened in the High Street in 1937 and served Dumbarton's gentlemen for 51 years. To make way for it the old Elephant Hotel, which had opened in 1762, was demolished in 1935. The property alongside the renovated Glencairn House was altered in 1922 by Woolworth who opened their local branch there. The upper portion of this property was replaced in 1939 when an extension was added.

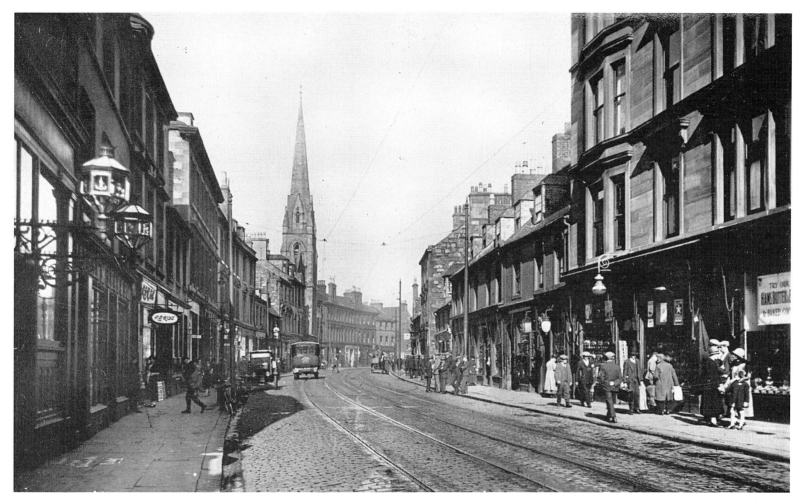

Initially known as the Free Church of Dumbarton, the Free High Church opened in 1864 on the site of the former Albert Shipyard. A section of the congregation, however, later broke away and formed the North Free Church, at which time the Free Church changed its name. Many of the older properties on both sides of the street have long since been demolished, including those beside the church which were removed in the 1970s to allow re-construction of Riverside Lane. Previously, the lane had been called Brewery Lane because of the presence of the Crown Brewery but prior to this it was called Ferry Lane, or Boat Vennel, as travellers were ferried across the Leven at this point before Dumbarton Bridge was built.

Bridge Street, Dumbarton.

M. 326

These older properties on Bridge Street, including the Cosy Corner Café at the corner with High Street, have long since been replaced by other buildings. Dumbarton Picture House stood on High Street near Risk Street, approximately opposite the Café, and no doubt cinemagoers were regular customers! Out of picture to the right was the industrial area known as the Artisan. This, like College Park Street, was swept away to allow the construction of the by-pass road, opened in 1974, which takes traffic over the River Leven on the Artisan Bridge. The only surviving older property west of Bridge Street is the Salvation Army Citadel, built in 1937.

In this tranquil view of the River Leven, the boaters have rowed out from Dumbarton Quay and are making their way up-river towards the Dumbarton (or Leven) Bridge. The need for a bridge over the Leven was first raised in 1682, and many times thereafter, as the river effectively cut off Argyll from the rest of Scotland. The original proposal was to build a bridge a few miles upstream at Bonhill, but Dumbarton citizens successfully lobbied the Duke of Argyll – who regularly went through Dumbarton on his way to his Castle at Inveraray – to site the bridge where it now stands. Construction of the bridge by a Dumbarton builder, John Brown, began in 1754 (although stones had been set aside for this purpose many years previously) and it was completed in 1765.

One of the areas most affected by modern redevelopment has been the Dumbarton Quay properties (including the Dumbarton Amateur Rowing Club premises) pictured here east of what was then Brewery Lane. In the 1960s, old buildings which had not been demolished already were pulled down to make way for the riverside walkway which was extended in 1972 to Dumbarton Bridge. In earlier times the Quay had been a bustling quarter. For example, local steamers provided a regular service between Dumbarton and Glasgow and many special excursions departed from the Quay, taking passengers along much of the coast of the Firth of Clyde. An 1887 advertisement for the Dumbarton steamer *PS Leven* states that 'The Leven steam package will sail from Dumbarton on Friday, 10th day of August, calling at Port Glasgow, Greenock, Gourock, Largs, Ardrossan, Irvine, Troon and Ayr. At the latter place she will remain that night giving passengers ample opportunity for viewing Burns cottage, his monument, the old Brig of Doon and Alloway Kirk'.

Pictured here across the Leven are the suburbs known as West Bridgend and Dennystown. West Bridgend was originally within the neighbouring parish of Cardross but was brought into the burgh after the opening of Dumbarton Bridge, while Dennystown was created in 1853 by William Denny when he had houses built there for his workers. Although these houses were small and lacked proper sanitation, they were considered an improvement on the crowded tenements in the burgh's vennels. Dennystown included Henryshott which, because of its large Irish population, was known locally as Wee Dublin. The nearby football pitch was known as Phoenix Park for similar reasons. By the turn of this century Dennystown was in need of regeneration and in the 1920s a small tenement in West Bridgend (ironically called Sunnybank!) became the subject of the burgh's first slum clearance scheme.

In earlier times horse racing, curling and skating were all popular sports in the district. The first organised sport, however, was rowing which started on Loch Lomond in 1828, one year prior to the commencement of the Oxford v Cambridge Boat Race. The first Dumbarton Regatta took place in 1830. Early races were held at high tide on the flooded Broad Meadow with the finish post placed opposite the College Bow which was then at its original site in College Park. At low tide foot and horse races were also held, making the entire event an important occasion in the social calendar. For a period the regattas ceased to take place and when they were restarted in 1853 the races were held on the Leven between the Castle and Dalreoch. Dumbarton Amateur Rowing Club, the local club, was founded in 1873 and well into this century Dumbarton and Vale of Leven crews monopolised the Scottish championships.

The opening of Dumbarton Bridge allowed well-to-do citizens such as the Dennys and Macmillans to build spacious mansions on the opposite bank of the river, well away from the old burgh, at Levengrove, Kirktonhill and at Clerkhill on land overlooking the River Clyde. These mansions included Levengrove House, Levenford House and Helenslee. The example of the wealthy shipbuilders was followed by other businessmen and traders who, besides building their villas in the same areas, also built at Comelybank and Oxhill. From 1853 working class families also moved across the Leven, but to the new suburb of Dennystown. In an attempt to alleviate overcrowding in the town in more recent times, large housing estates have been built further along Cardross Road at Brucehill and Castlehill. Castlehill is situated on the site of the estate where Robert the Bruce spent the last years of his life.

Levengrove Park, Dumbarton.

In 1880 the shipbuilders Peter Denny and John Macmillan bought Levengrove Estate for £20,000 with the intention of creating a public park for Dumbarton. It was ready in 1885 and a public holiday was declared to allow as many of the townsfolk as possible to attend the official opening ceremony. Within the park are the remains of the former Parish Church of Cardross which fell within Dumbarton Parish when the parish boundary was extended west of the River Leven in 1644. The church, which measured only 40 feet by 20 feet, was at one time under the jurisdiction of Glasgow Cathedral. A cluster of houses around it was called Kirkton of Cardross, a name recalled by the suburb of Kirktonhill which is situated to the north of the park.

The eighteenth century Levengrove House was once the home of the Dixons of Levengrove who owned the Dumbarton Glassworks. Situated in what later became Levengrove Park, it was one of several large houses built on the west bank of the Leven. When Robert Burns visited Dumbarton in 1787 he stayed at the house as the guest of its then owner, John MacAulay, the Town Clerk. By all accounts Burns enjoyed a rapturous reception in Dumbarton and was made a freeman of the burgh, although one local minister, James Oliphant, protested strongly at this honour as he felt that Burns had previously ridiculed him. The Burgess Ticket presented to Burns on that historic occasion was later given by a descendant of the poet to the Dumbarton Burns Club, who in turn presented it to the town in 1926. Levengrove was demolished in the early 1880s.

Levenford House on Helenslee Road is another of the many fine mansions associated with the Dumbarton shipbuilding families. Commissioned by James Denny, the house was built in 1853 in the Scottish baronial style. The architect was John Thomas Rochead, who also designed Dennystown for William Denny. In the 1860s the house became the residence of Walter Brock, one time chairman of Denny, who enlarged it. After Brock's death in 1907 it passed to his son, Walter Junior, and daughter Ellen, and in 1937 Walter Junior's widow presented it to Dunbarton County Council for use as a library or museum. The house was the Dunbarton County Libraries Headquarters for many years and is presently the headquarters of West Dunbartonshire Libraries. Another building associated with the family was the Brock Baths on the Common, opened in 1914 as a memorial to Walter Senior. The site is now occupied by the Meadow Leisure Centre.

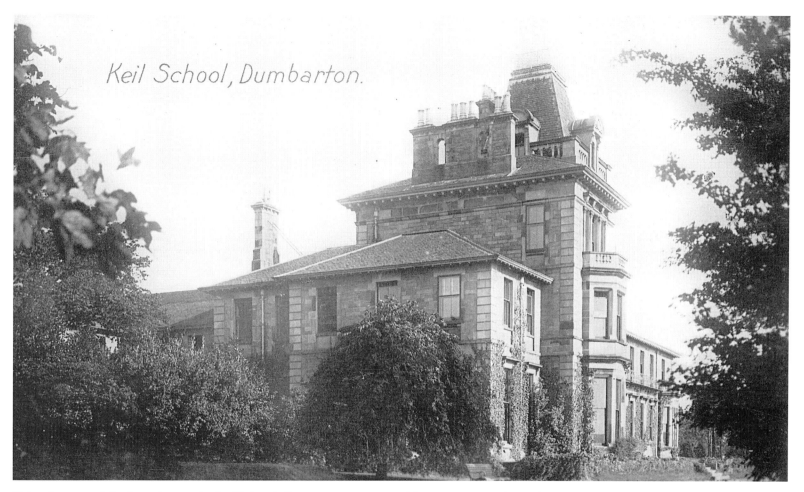

Keil School, Dumbarton.

Helenslee, one of the finest houses in the Kirktonhill area, was constructed between 1856 and 1858 for the shipbuilder, Dr Peter Denny. The house was situated on high ground facing the river and, like Levenford House, was designed by the architect John Thomas Rochead. In 1925, Helenslee and its grounds were purchased to house Keil School whose premises at Southend in Kintyre had been destroyed by fire in 1924. The school owes its origin to Sir William Mackinnon of Campbeltown, the founder of the British India Steam Navigation Company and the Imperial British East Africa Trading Company, who set up a trust 'to provide education for deserving Highland lads'. A bronze statue of Sir William stands to the side of Keil's South House.

"NOTRE DAME" HIGH SCHOOL FOR GIRLS, DUMBARTON.

The Notre Dame Roman Catholic School for girls was established at Clerkhill in 1912 following a request by Monsignor Hugh Kelly to Notre Dame House in Namur, France, for teaching assistance for his parish. The building pictured is the original school which was built alongside Notre Dame Convent. By 1969, however, this building had fallen into disuse and a new Notre Dame School was opened on the opposite side of Cardross Road, further west of the boys-only St Patrick's School (which had opened in 1927). In 1990 the two schools merged to form Our Lady and St Patrick's School, and later the old St Patrick's School was demolished and a new St Michael's Primary School was built on its site.

County Hospital, Dumbarton.

Originally a Fever and Infectious Diseases hospital, the County Hospital (now called 'Dumbarton Joint') replaced the former Combination Hospital. Pictured is the main building which opened in 1894 at a cost of around £20,000. It occupied a five acre site, then outside the burgh boundary, on an isolated area off Cardross Road. It is said that one method used to stop the spread of infectious diseases was to quarantine patients within its hermetically sealed observation wards! Non-infectious diseases were treated at the Cottage Hospital. This was opened in 1890 on ground beside Dumbarton Common which was purchased from the trustees of the estate of the late William Denny and handed over to the Dumbarton Social Union to be run as a voluntary hospital.

The Bridge, Dumbarton

This 1909 view of Dumbarton Bridge, looking towards High Street and the Gospel Hall, shows the No.14 Dumbarton Burgh & County open-top tram on its Dalmuir run. This route went into operation in 1908 when the tramway system was extended eastward beyond the burgh boundary at Dumbuck through the villages of Milton, Bowling, Old Kilpatrick and Dalmuir. Given that the tramway company was especially dependent on the holiday trade, this route was an obvious development as it allowed the Burgh & County trams to link up with the Glasgow Corporation trams at the wooden bascule bridge crossing the Forth and Clyde Canal at Dalmuir. At this point Glaswegians heading for Balloch and Loch Lomond would transfer from Corporation trams by disembarking, walking across the bridge and re-embarking on Dumbarton trams. This route proved immensely popular and 49,000 passengers made the journey in just one week in 1908!

The bridge in 1936, again looking towards the High Street with the steeple of the Free High Church on the right. Over the years the bridge has been renovated several times, principally in 1884 (when it was widened and footpaths constructed) and in 1934 (when the entire structure was strengthened with reinforced concrete). In the foreground on both sides of the bridge are Matthew Paul's Boiler and Engine Works. Over the bridge to the left, behind the Gospel Hall, is the beginning of the Artisan which stood on the site of the old Dumbarton Glassworks. The Glassworks were started in 1777 and later taken over by the Dixon family, one of whom, Jacob Dixon, was provost of both Dumbarton and Helensburgh. In 1831 both Jacob and his son died within days of each other and the Glassworks were closed until 1837 when they reopened under James Christie. They closed again in 1850.

The Municipal Buildings were built between 1900 and 1904 and are situated in College Park which is near the site of the medieval Collegiate Church. Also within the grounds of the park was College Park House which was originally the property of John Macmillan, another of Dumbarton's shipbuilding giants, and, later, Sheriff Campbell, whose grand-nephew Lord Overtoun gifted the College Park Estate to Dumbarton. Various artefacts stand in the grounds of the Municipal Buildings, including the College Bow and the three cannons known as MacFarlan's Hurdies or Hurdles. These cannons were reputedly brought from Burma and presented to Provost Robert MacFarlan who, in turn, gifted them to the town after the opening of the Municipal Buildings in 1902.

In this turn of the century view of Strathleven Place, at its junction with College Park Street, the tramway tracks can be seen leading north towards Barloan Toll. The buildings on the left-hand side of the street, including the chemist shop, were replaced by the public library in 1910, which was built with the assistance of a grant from Andrew Carnegie, the Dunfermline-born steel magnate and benefactor of libraries. In the mid-1800s, William Denny had offered to part-finance a subscription library if the balance was met by the working men of the burgh, but his idea was not supported. However, at a meeting of ratepayers in 1881 it was agreed to form a public library. This was initially located in Heggie's Building in the High Street and then, in 1892, in the ground floor of the Denny Institute. When these premises proved inadequate, the present site was acquired.

Dumbarton's first school was the Grammar School which is referred to in a charter dating from 1485. At one time the school was located in a room in the tower of the Parish Church in High Street, but in 1788 a two-storey building in Church Street was erected by public subscription. When this building proved inadequate, a new school – thereafter known as the Burgh Academy – was opened opposite, in front of the Burgh Hall. In 1914 the building pictured here was opened at Braehead on a raised site at the head of the Common. In the 1950s the former Model Yachting Pond on the Common, which had been filled in just before the Second World War, was used as playing fields for the Academy. Pupils from the Academy transferred to Hartfield Secondary School in nearby Crosslet Road in the 1970s and the building then became Braehead Primary School.

Nowadays Dumbuck Hotel is a family-run hotel, strategically located on Glasgow Road on the eastern approaches to Dumbarton, just west of a major road junction directing visitors to Helensburgh and Loch Lomond. The site once formed part of the estate of Dumbuck (formerly part of the ancient Barony of Colquhoun) which was sold by Sir Charles Edmonstone of Duntreath to General Thomas Geils and it was the Geils family who built the house as a family mansion in 1824. In the 1920s it was purchased and converted by Babcock & Wilcox for use by their staff but the company sold it in 1936. Since then it has been extensively modernised but without, however, losing its historical character and 'B' listed status. The grounds immediately west of the hotel on Glasgow Road were laid out by Babcock & Wilcox as a recreation ground for their staff.

Murroch Glen is situated on the lower slopes of Dumbarton Muir to the north of Dumbarton. Once it afforded fine views eastwards to the Lang Crags and southwards to the River Clyde and Dumbarton Rock, but the post-war Bellsmyre housing estate has since rather diminished the view towards the River. In the early years of this century the glen was the site of the annual 'Glen Concert', an event which first started in 1904 and continued to be staged until the 1950s.